HERACLES THE HERO

Contents

Welcome to Rigby Navigator

Giving you the Right Tools for the Job

Rigby Navigator is specially designed to help you unlock the potential of guided reading. It makes guided reading easy to manage and enjoyable for both teachers and children. The programme provides books for fiction, non-fiction, poetry and plays for 7–11 year olds. *Navigator* can also be used alongside your existing guided reading resources.

Navigator Fiction

Rigby Navigator Fiction has been written to help you deliver creative and effective guided reading sessions for all your pupils. Each book contains three short stories, tailor-made for guided reading sessions, so they are the right length and at the right interest level. Each book is supported by its own Teaching Guide. The clear teaching focus for each session will save you valuable preparation time.

Developing Comprehension Skills

Guided reading is an important part of children's literacy experience. It is an opportunity for them to engage with the reading process and to discuss their thoughts with the teacher and with other children. It helps ensure that they experience a broad variety of texts, genres and vocabulary. Guided reading in KS2 helps children to build on their literal comprehension and factual recall skills. In addition, it supports the development of the higher level skills of inference, deduction, justification and evaluation. Throughout the *Rigby Navigator* sessions, questions are provided to help children acquire and develop these skills and allow teachers opportunities to assess pupils' progress across the range of Assessment Focuses for Reading.

Implementing Guided Reading

All schools have different timetables and priorities, and guided reading should be considered as part of a whole school literacy programme. Many schools find it most effective to include some guided reading time in the main literacy session, with extra daily guided reading sessions. *Rigby Navigator* provides plenty of materials for groups to work on while the teacher works with a particular set of children.

You can choose your own route through the material, so that you can personalise your sessions to meet particular groups' needs.

Making the Most of Guided Reading

Each session in *Rigby Navigator* details the Primary Framework objectives, as well as success criteria. These can be shared with the children at the start of each session, to make sure that they know what each session will cover. Recapping the success criteria at the end of the session will encourage children to evaluate their own performance.

Support for Planning

Each session in *Rigby Navigator* lists the Primary Framework objectives covered in that session; and these are summarised in the table opposite, alongside the Assessment Focuses. Charts showing which of the Primary Framework objectives are and are not covered for a given year are available in the *Rigby Navigator* Programme Handbooks.

Support for Assessment

Valuable information can be accrued during guided reading about children's application of essential reading skills and strategies. Each *Rigby Navigator* session identifies a main Assessment Focus for Reading with related target questions and model responses, tailored to each book, to help teachers to assess children's responses. Levelling Guidance Sheets can be found at the end of the Teacher's Guide. Please note that this should just form *part* of the evidence you should gather in assessing your children.

Differentiation

The wide range of ability levels in the classroom adds to the time needed to prepare for effective guided reading. *Navigator* Teaching Guides offer teachers flexible routes through each story, so that each guided reading session can be differentiated, allowing you to meet every group's needs.

Models for Writing

The short stories also serve as perfect exemplar texts for children's own writing. The Guides have a strong focus on writing, drawing on the essential link between reading and writing.

Primary Framework Teaching Objectives and Assessment Opportunities

Heracles the Hero – Greek Legends

		Session 1 / 2	Session 3 / 4
How Heracles Cleaned the Stables of King Augeus	**Primary Framework Objectives**	**Focus on Characters in a Legend/Hero and Foe** **Y5 Strand 7: 1** Use evidence from a text to explain ideas **Y5 Strand 7: 3** Compare structure of different types of text **Y5 Strand 9: 2** Write own story; experiment with different styles	**Focus on Author's Techniques** **Y5 Strand 7: 1** Use evidence from a text to explain ideas **Y5 Strand 7: 5** Explore how writers produce dramatic effects
	AFs	**AF 2** Understand, describe, select or retrieve information, events or ideas from texts and use quotation and reference to text **AF 4*** Identify and comment on the structure and organisation of texts, including grammatical and presentational features at text level **AF 5** Explain and comment on writers' use of language, including grammatical and literary features at word and sentence level	**AF 5*** Explain and comment on writers' use of language, including grammatical and literary features at word and sentence level **AF 6** Identify and comment on writers' purposes and viewpoints and the overall effect on the reader
The Golden Apples of the Hesperides	**Primary Framework Objectives**	**Focus on Style** **Y5 Strand 7: 1** Use evidence from a text to explain ideas **Y5 Strand 7: 3** Compare structure of different types of text	**Focus on Points of View** **Y5 Strand 7: 2** Infer writers' perspectives **Y5 Strand 7: 3** Compare structure of different types of text **Y5 Strand 8: 2** Compare usefulness of visualisation/prediction/empathy in exploring texts **Y5 Strand 9: 4** Use direct/reported speech, action and detail to vary pace/develop viewpoint
	AFs	**AF 4** As above **AF 5** As above **AF 7*** Relate texts to their social, cultural and historical traditions	**AF 3** Deduce, infer or interpret information, events or ideas from texts **AF 4*** As above
Heracles in the Underworld	**Primary Framework Objectives**	**Focus on Inference** **Y5 Strand 7: 1** Use evidence from a text to explain ideas **Y5 Strand 8: 2** Compare usefulness of visualisation/prediction/empathy in exploring texts	**Focus on Language** **Y5 Strand 7: 2** Infer writers' perspectives **Y5 Strand 7: 5** Explore how writer's produce dramatic effects **Y5 Strand 9: 4** Use direct/reported speech, action and detail to vary pace/develop viewpoint
	AFs	**AF 2*** As above **AF 3** As above	**AF 4** As above **AF 5** As above **AF 6*** As above

How to Use the Navigator Fiction Teaching Guides

The *Navigator* Teaching Guides offer flexible routes through the stories for guided reading. The Guides put you in control of guided reading, as you choose the routes through the material depending on the needs of your children. Each session can be held over one or two days, as fits your timetable and the progress of your guided reading groups.

Session 1 / 2

At a Glance

This section will save you valuable time, by giving an overview of the story as well as highlighting the literacy opportunities in the text.

Independent reading

Depending on a group's ability, some children may be able to read the story ahead of the guided reading session. This section contains ideas of areas children could look out for or focus on as they read the text.

Text introduction

This short, focused section introduces the story to the children, and activates the prior knowledge and experience that they bring to the reading.

Teaching strategies

During this part of the session, children are supported in their reading and response to the text.

- The boxed questions enable you to assess how well the children have understood the story, and provide an opportunity to gather evidence for a particular Assessment Focus. For these questions, Levelling Guidance Sheets are provided at the end of the Teacher's Guide. Other assessment opportunities are identified throughout the session and are shown by the (AF) symbol.
- **Going deeper:** These focused questions lead the children deeper into the text. They must support their views with evidence from the text. These sections encourage children to develop a range of comprehension skills:
  - *Prediction*: encouraging children to use their knowledge of the story so far to predict what might happen next.
  - *Constructing images*: asking children to visualise what is happening in the story, leading them to a close analysis of the text.
  - *Questioning*: modelling questions that children might ask of each other, the author, or themselves.
  - *Text-structure analysis*: expanding children's awareness of how texts are structured.
  - *Sequencing texts*: applying knowledge about how texts are put together.
  - *Semantic strategies*: supporting children in decoding unfamiliar words.
  - *Interpretive strategies*: enhancing critical analysis skills, including inference and deduction, and reading between the lines.
  - *Monitoring understanding*: encouraging children to reflect on their own understanding of the text.
- **Focus on:** This section focuses on a number of pages in the story and fulfils a key objective. Often this focused questioning requires children to read between and beyond the lines of the text.

Respond and return

Now the children reflect in detail on the text they have read. This is also an opportunity to consolidate the strategies used.

Follow-up

The PCM relates to the **Going deeper, Focus on** and/or **Respond and return** sections and usually has a reading or writing focus.

Challenge: Differentiation
The main stem of the session is the same for all children. You can choose from the range of literacy activities available according to the group you are taking. As a guided reading session progresses faster with more able children, the Challenge sections extend the main stem of the session and build on the teaching that has gone before.

Session 3 / 4

Session 3 / 4 works in the same way as Session 1 / 2, but may have different learning objectives and Assessment Focuses. Depending on how fast children progress, you could ask them to complete the follow-up PCM (which always has a writing focus) in the next session. Additional writing suggestions are also given.

Activates children's prior knowledge

Page numbers refer to pupil books

A focused look at the text

Story synopsis

Main assessment opportunity for the session – levelling guidance sheets provided

Gives you the literacy focus of the story – saving you time

Encourages critical thinking

Success criteria to discuss with children before and after the session

Other assessment opportunity

Assessment Focuses for the sessions

Questions and areas to look out for as children read the text for the first time

Differentiated routes through the material put you in control

Focused follow-up ideas

Consolidates strategies used

Strong link to writing in Session 3 / 4

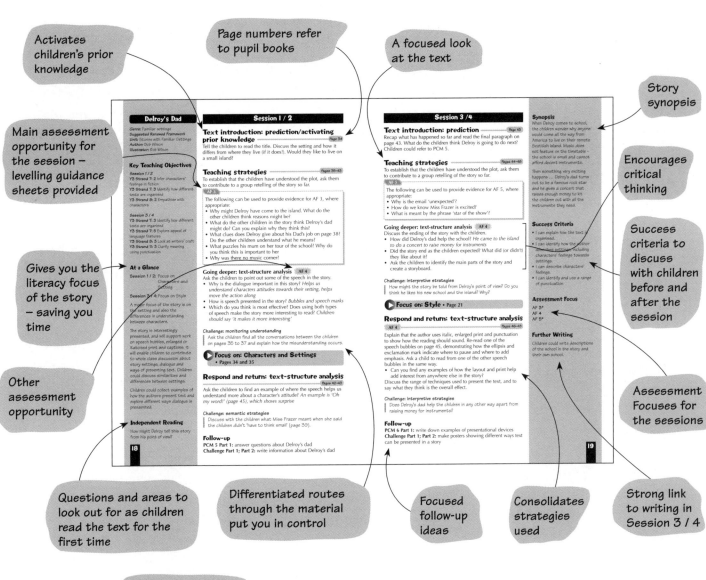

Focus section for both sessions

Annotated pages put you in control

Focused question prompts

All children complete Part 1, and more able children also complete Part 2

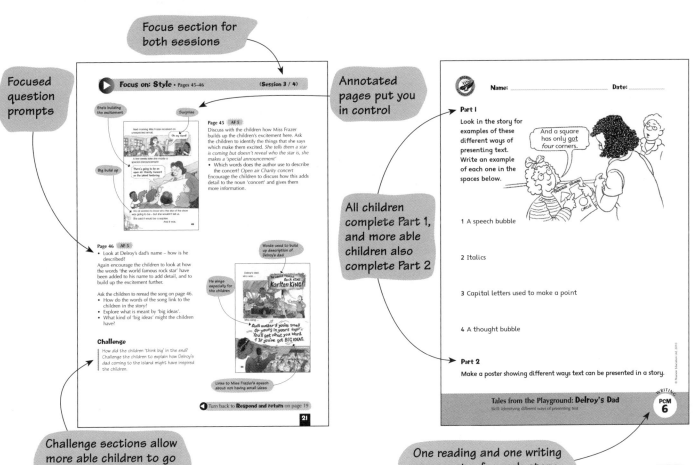

Challenge sections allow more able children to go even deeper into the text

One reading and one writing copymaster for each story

How Heracles Cleaned the Stables of King Augeas

Genre: Greek legend
**Suggested Renewed Framework
Unit:** Traditional stories, fables, myths, legends
Author: Antonia Barber
Illustrator: Peter Doherty

Key Teaching Objectives

Session 1 / 2
Y5 Strand 7: 1 Use evidence from a text to explain ideas
Y5 Strand 7: 3 Compare structure of different types of text
Y5 Strand 9: 2 Write own story: experiment with different styles

Session 3 / 4
Y5 Strand 7: 1 Use evidence from a text to explain ideas
Y5 Strand 7: 5 Explore how writers use language to produce dramatic effects

At a Glance

Session 1 / 2: Focus on Characters in a Legend/Hero and Foe
Session 3 / 4: Focus on Author's Techniques

Based on the legends of Ancient Greece, the book retells three of the labours of Heracles. The story has a straightforward problem/resolution structure and many familiar features of legends, particularly in the characters.

Independent Reading

As you read, look for anything that reminds you of other legends you have read.

Text introduction: prediction/activating prior knowledge
Pages 5–7

Look at the cover and title page. Ask the children what 'retold' means. Explain that the book contains three stories about a hero, Heracles, from an Ancient Greek legend. Ask a child to read pages 5–7 and demonstrate using page 62 to check pronunciation of unfamiliar names. Ask the children: who was Hera and why did she want to punish Zeus?

Teaching strategies
Pages 9–15, 60–63

To establish that the children have understood the plot, ask them to contribute to a group retelling of the story so far.

AF 4

The following can be used to gather evidence for AF 4, where appropriate:
- Why does the writer start with the introduction rather than going straight into the first story?
- Before describing the fifth task, the writer tells us about tasks 1 to 4. Why do you think this is?
- What is the purpose of pages 60–61?
- How does the layout on pages 62–63 make the pronunciation guide easy to use?

Going deeper: text-structure analysis
Ask the children to describe the first four tasks given to Heracles. What is the familiar pattern to each of these stories? *Trial set; hero overcomes fantastical beast; returns to cheering crowds*
- Are there any differences to this basic pattern? *Third task is more complex; takes longer; involves help from goddess Artemis*

Challenge: interpretive strategies
Rate the challenges of Heracles from most to least difficult using evidence from the text.

 Focus on: Characters in a Legend/Hero and Foe • Pages 10 and 14

Respond and return: relating text to prior reading experience

Discuss with the children typical features of legends (e.g. great hero, improbable feats, challenges to overcome, fantastical creatures). Encourage them to make links to any other legends they have read (e.g. St George and the dragon).

Challenge: interpretive strategies
Ask children to compare a legend with a fable or myth.

Follow-up

PCM 1 Part 1: write their own version of one of the labours
Challenge Part 1; Part 2: find out more about the gods on Mount Olympus

Text introduction: monitoring understanding/prediction — Page 15

Recap the story and discuss the latest task. Ask the children to predict what might happen. Remind the children that these legends have been passed down through generations (first orally and then written down). Discuss how this affects how the story is told.

Teaching strategies — Pages 16–24

To establish that the children have understood the plot, ask them to contribute to a group retelling of the story.

AF 5

The following can be used to gather evidence for AF 5, where appropriate:
- Which words and phrases on page 16 suggest that you are reading a story set a long time ago?
- Read the dialogue between characters. Which parts suggest that this is not a modern story?
- How does the choice of words help to create the horror of the stables?

Going deeper: interpretive strategies

Discuss how words and phrases might be changed into more familiar modern language. How might we say these today?
- '... could not compensate for the foul stench ...'
- '... how could it possibly be accomplished in a single day?'
- '... even though his destination was still some distance away in an adjacent valley.'

Challenge: interpretive strategies/genre exchange

If you were telling this story orally, how would it be different?

 Focus on: Author's Techniques • Pages 21–22

Respond and return: interpretive strategies **AF 6**

Ask the children if their predictions were right. Discuss how Heracles needed to use cleverness as well as strength to succeed.
- What is the story trying to say? *Trials can be tests of intelligence and skill as well as strength; sometimes we have to overcome seemingly impossible difficulties in life*
- Do you think this is effective?

Challenge: interpretive strategies

How would you rate this task: more difficult or less difficult than the earlier ones? What makes you say that?

Follow-up

PCM 2 Part 1: notes on the main stages in the story
Challenge Part 1; Part 2: identify key points in the story; writing a speech

Synopsis

Based on the legends of Ancient Greece, the book retells three of the labours of Heracles. The introduction sets the scene and provides background to why Heracles was given the labours. In the first of the stories Heracles is set a seemingly impossible task which is without glory. The story tells how Heracles uses his strength and cleverness to clean the stables of King Augeas.

Success Criteria

- I can identify typical characters, events, themes and story patterns in legends.
- I can refer to the text to support my comments about characters and genre.
- I can talk about how a writer uses language to build up/ describe events effectively.
- I can plan an alternative version of a story in the same style.

Assessment Focus

AF 2
AF 4*
AF 5*
AF 6

Further Writing

Write the conversation between Heracles and King Augeas after Heracles had cleaned the stables.

Page 10 AF 2

Ask the children to identify the different characters and their role in the legend: the brave hero, the challenge of ferocious creatures and fantastical beasts, the opponent or enemy. (See annotations.)

- What are the characteristics of the hero Heracles? Refer to evidence on page 10 to support your ideas.
- Look at Heracles' actions and what these tell us about his character. *Immensely strong, brave, popular*

Ask the children to look for further evidence about the characteristics of Heracles by going back through pages 11–13. Can they find evidence of any new characteristics in what we are told or his actions (e.g. kindness and gentleness using evidence from page 12)?

Look at how the writer describes the fantastical beasts in some detail.

- Why is it important? (e.g. *to make them sound really fearsome, a worthy challenge; to emphasise Heracles' strength and bravery*)

What are the characteristics of Eurytheus, Heracles' enemy? Refer to evidence on page 10.

Fantastical beasts or monsters

Heracles is the strong, brave hero

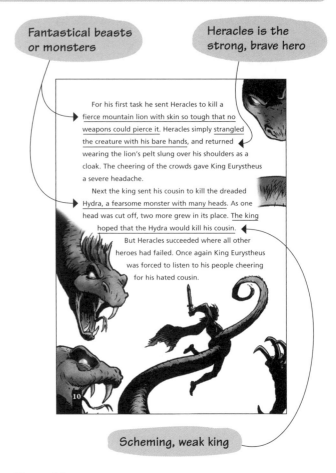

For his first task he sent Heracles to kill a fierce mountain lion with skin so tough that no weapons could pierce it. Heracles simply strangled the creature with his bare hands, and returned wearing the lion's pelt slung over his shoulders as a cloak. The cheering of the crowds gave King Eurystheus a severe headache.

Next the king sent his cousin to kill the dreaded Hydra, a fearsome monster with many heads. As one head was cut off, two more grew in its place. The king hoped that the Hydra would kill his cousin.

But Heracles succeeded where all other heroes had failed. Once again King Eurystheus was forced to listen to his people cheering for his hated cousin.

Scheming, weak king

Page 14

Ask the children to give their judgements on Eurytheus' character based on this event.

- What do his actions tell us about him?
- What about others' reactions to him?

Ask them to refer to evidence from the text to support their views. (See annotations.)

Discuss the relationship between Eurytheus and Heracles.

- What does Eurytheus think of Heracles?
- What does Heracles think of Eurytheus?
- What makes you say that?

Ask children to re-read page 9 to find further evidence about the relationship between Eurytheus and Heracles.

Challenge

What do other people think about Eurytheus and Heracles? What evidence is there in the text to support your ideas?

Angry because he's been humiliated

Cowardly

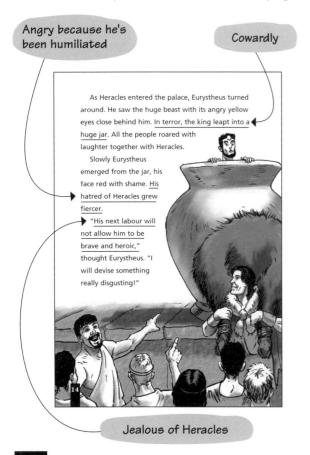

As Heracles entered the palace, Eurystheus turned around. He saw the huge beast with its angry yellow eyes close behind him. In terror, the king leapt into a huge jar. All the people roared with laughter together with Heracles.

Slowly Eurystheus emerged from the jar, his face red with shame. His hatred of Heracles grew fiercer.

"His next labour will not allow him to be brave and heroic," thought Eurystheus. "I will devise something really disgusting!"

Jealous of Heracles

Turn back to **Respond and return** on page 6

Then as he watched, an ingenious plan came to him. He had thought of a way to clean out the stables in a single day. Better still, it could be done without soiling his hands!

Leaving the clean animals to roam free, Heracles made his way down to a point just above the stable yard. Here he began to pick up huge rocks that no other man could have lifted. Carrying them upon his back he started to build a wall. He worked for many hours without respite. As the wall grew, it made a dam, trapping the waters of the two rivers. The dam rose higher and higher.

When the wall reached above his head, Heracles was satisfied. He left it and began another task. Still using only his bare hands, he tore huge rocks out of the ground. He made a deep gully running from the foot of the dam to the back of the stable. Then he made a very large gap in the stable wall.

Details that add to the drama

Main events – these need to be present in any vision

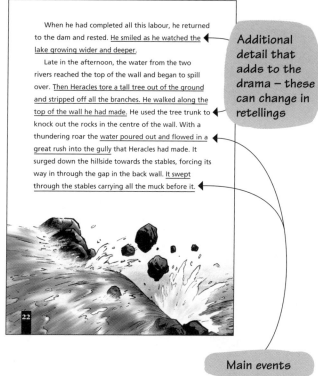

When he had completed all this labour, he returned to the dam and rested. He smiled as he watched the lake growing wider and deeper.

Late in the afternoon, the water from the two rivers reached the top of the wall and began to spill over. Then Heracles tore a tall tree out of the ground and stripped off all the branches. He walked along the top of the wall he had made. He used the tree trunk to knock out the rocks in the centre of the wall. With a thundering roar the water poured out and flowed in a great rush into the gully that Heracles had made. It surged down the hillside towards the stables, forcing its way in through the gap in the back wall. It swept through the stables carrying all the muck before it.

Additional detail that adds to the drama – these can change in retellings

Main events

Pages 21 and 22 (AF 5)

Ask some of the children to tell in their own words how Heracles managed to achieve the task of cleaning the stables. Then re-read pages 21–22.

Discuss the differences between the written version and the children's retelling and remind the children that it is the author's job to embellish the main events.

- Identify the main events and the details added to build up the drama. (See annotations.)

Look at how the author hides the 'ingenious plan' from the reader to keep us guessing what Heracles is doing with the rocks and how he plans to clean the stables.

- Which words and phrases make it sound like a real labour that only Heracles could accomplish? *Huge rocks that no other man could have lifted; using only his bare hands*

Ask one of the children to read aloud the end of page 22 (describing what happens when Heracles makes a hole in the dam wall).

- How does the writer build this event up and make it sound dramatic? *Discuss use of descriptive detail; choice of vocabulary; use of repetition ('it surged' … 'it swept')*

What are the words and phrases used to describe the movement of the water? *'Surged'; 'forcing'; 'thundering roar'; 'a great rush'*

- Why were these chosen? *To suggest the power and sudden force of the water*

Challenge

Make up some additional descriptive details to add even more to the drama of the event.

◀ Turn back to **Respond and return** on page 7

9

Part 1

Write your own version of how Heracles captured the wild boar and carried it back to Mycenae. Use this prompt sheet to help you.

Opening:

_____
_____
_____

Complication:

_____
_____
_____

Climax:

_____
_____
_____

Resolution and ending:

_____
_____
_____

Part 2

Find out more about Zeus, Hera and the gods on Mount Olympus. Write a fact file.

PCM 1

READING

Heracles the Hero: **How Heracles Cleaned the Stables of King Augeus** Skill: Writing a version of Heracles capturing the wild boar

Part 1

Jot down the key events from each part of the story. Use your notes as prompts to tell the story to a partner.

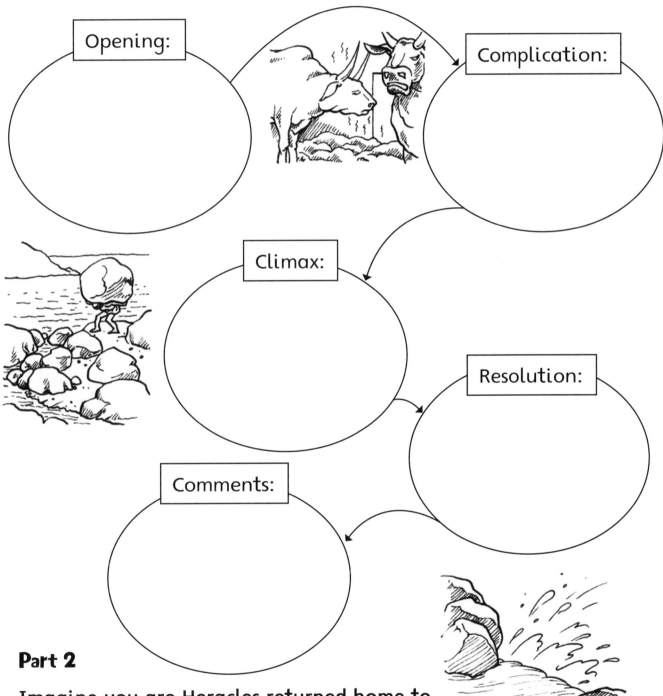

Opening:

Complication:

Climax:

Resolution:

Comments:

Part 2

Imagine you are Heracles returned home to Mycenae. Write a speech to impress the gathered crowd about how you cleaned out the stables.

Heracles the Hero: How Heracles Cleaned the Stables of King Augeus Skills: Identifying key points in the story; Writing a speech

WRITING

PCM **2**

The Golden Apples of the Hesperides

Genre: Greek legend
Suggested Renewed Framework Unit: Traditional stories, fables, myths, legends
Author: Antonia Barber
Illustrator: Peter Doherty

Key Teaching Objectives

Session 1 / 2
Y5 Strand 7: 1 Use evidence from the text to explain ideas
Y5 Strand 7: 3 Compare structure of different types of text

Session 3 / 4
Y5 Strand 7: 2 Infer writers' perspectives
Y5 Strand 7: 3 Compare structure of different types of text
Y5 Strand 8: 2 Compare usefulness of visualisation/prediction/empathy in exploring texts.
Y5 Strand 9: 4 Use direct/reported speech, action and detail to vary pace/develop viewpoint

At a Glance

Session 1 / 2: Focus on Style
Session 3 / 4: Focus on Points of View

The story shows how Heracles succeeds in his task through bravery and kindness and adds to our understanding of the character.

The story exemplifies many of the typical features of legends found in the first story but it has a more complex 'quest' style plot structure with a number of complications along the way. This makes it useful for identifying similarities and differences between the two stories.

Independent reading

How is this story like a quest? Make notes to keep track of key events or represent the story structure.

Text introduction: monitoring understanding/prediction
Page 25

Recap the first story and discuss the key features of legends. Read the title and turn to page 60 to find the task they are going to read about. Ask children to read page 25 which sets the scene for the new story. What might be dangerous or impossible about this task? What might it involve?

Teaching strategies
Pages 25–33

To establish that the children have understood the plot, ask them to contribute to a group retelling of the story so far.

AF 7

The following can be used to gather evidence for AF 7, where appropriate:
- How could you tell this was a legend just from reading pages 25–26?
- What are we told about where these events take place?
- How does the pattern of the story compare to the first story?
- How are the characters different in this story?

Going deeper: visualising; text-structure analysis **AF 4**

Discuss how the structure of this story is longer and more complex than the first: movements in setting and time; a series of vital encounters with different characters; a series of problems to be overcome; like a quest.
Ask children to make a story map to help them visualise and keep track of the story. Mark on it the places and people he meets and make notes about the key event and significance of each encounter.

Challenge: interpretive strategies

Discuss the role played by gods and goddesses in the two stories read so far. Are the gods kind or cruel? Ask the children to find evidence from both stories to support their opinions.

▶ Focus on: Style • Pages 30–31

Respond and return: relate to own experiences

What does this story tell us about Heracles' character that we didn't know before? *He's compassionate as well as brave and strong* Discuss the characteristics that we look for in heroes of today, encouraging children to talk about people who show determination, compassion and bravery.

Challenge: interpretive strategies

What would Nereus and Prometheus say about Heracles? Encourage them to use evidence from the text to support their ideas.

Follow-up

PCM 3 Part 1: identify Heracles' different qualities
Challenge Part 1; Part 2: writing about three of those qualities

Text introduction: monitoring understanding/prediction
Page 33

Ask children to use their story map notes to recap Heracles' quest so far, describing the complications and who has helped him along the way.
- Which problems have been solved so far?
- What problems remain?

Teaching strategies
Pages 34–41

To establish that the children have understood the plot, ask them to contribute to a group retelling of the story.

AF 4

The following can be used to gather evidence for AF 4, where appropriate:
- How is this story like a quest?
- Which words and phrases show how long the story takes?
- How is the structure of the story the same as the first story? How is it different?
- Why is the meeting with Atlas important in the story?

Going deeper: interpretive strategies/questioning   **AF 3**

Discuss the meeting between Atlas and Heracles (pages 34–37). Use questioning to explore children's understanding of the characters' thoughts and motives.
- 'I am sufficiently strong to hold up the heavens.' Why does Heracles say this?
- 'Atlas watched, fascinated.' Why was he fascinated?
- He did not like to admit that he found the weight a burden. Why not?

Challenge: interpretive strategies
Ask children to compare Atlas and Heracles using evidence from the text. Who is the strongest/cleverest/most patient/proudest?

 Focus on: Points of View • Pages 38–39

Respond and return: interpretive strategies
Pages 41–42

Ask the children to explain fully how the task is finally resolved and ends (with the apples safely back where they belong).
- Is it the right ending?
- What makes you say that?
- What if Heracles had not returned them?

Challenge: activating prior knowledge
Ask the children if they can think of any other quest-style stories.

Follow-up

PCM 4 Part 1: write about Atlas and Heracles' meeting
Challenge Part 1; Part 2: write about the encounter from Atlas' point of view

Synopsis

The second of the three stories describes the tenth task given to Heracles by his cousin. Eurytheus is jealous of Heracles and chooses a task that he thinks will anger Hera. He sends his cousin to bring back the golden apples of the Hesperides. The story shows how Heracles succeeds in his task through courage and kindness.

Success Criteria

- I can describe similarities and differences between two legends.
- I can make notes of the main events in a story.
- I can compare story structures and recognise complications and how they are resolved.
- I can imagine and explore events from different points of view.
- I can describe events from another character's point of view, including details and actions.

Assessment Focus

AF 3
AF 4*
AF 5
AF 7*

Further Writing

Write a postcard or letter from Atlas telling his friend Prometheus about his encounter with Heracles.

Formal, traditional storytelling language

Longer, more complex sentences

Different connecting devices

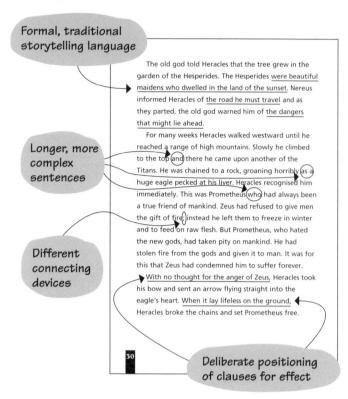

The old god told Heracles that the tree grew in the garden of the Hesperides. The Hesperides <u>were beautiful maidens who dwelled in the land of the sunset.</u> Nereus informed Heracles of <u>the road he must travel</u> and as they parted, the old god warned him of <u>the dangers that might lie ahead.</u>

For many weeks Heracles walked westward until he reached a range of high mountains. Slowly he climbed to the top and there he came upon another of the Titans. He was chained to a rock, groaning horribly as a huge eagle pecked at his liver. Heracles recognised him immediately. This was Prometheus who had always been a true friend of mankind. Zeus had refused to give men the gift of fire; instead he left them to freeze in winter and to feed on raw flesh. But Prometheus, who hated the new gods, had taken pity on mankind. He had stolen fire from the gods and given it to man. It was for this that Zeus had condemned him to suffer forever.

<u>With no thought for the anger of Zeus,</u> Heracles took his bow and sent an arrow flying straight into the eagle's heart. <u>When it lay lifeless on the ground,</u> Heracles broke the chains and set Prometheus free.

30

Deliberate positioning of clauses for effect

31

Pages 30 and 31 (AF 5)

Ask the children to find pages 30–31, look at the picture and tell this part of the story orally, taking it in turns round the group. Then ask some of the children to read page 30 aloud, a paragraph each.

• What is the difference between your oral retelling and the written version? *The amount of detail included; the language used; non-verbal aspects of oral storytelling*

Can you find examples of archaic or formal story language used on page 30? *'Dwelled'; 'the road he must travel'; 'dangers that lie ahead'; 'walked westward'; 'came upon'.*

Discuss how to transform some of the sentences into more natural language, e.g. Nereus told Heracles which way to go and warned him about the dangers he might face.

Explain that sentences also play a part in establishing the style or sound of a written story. Here the writer uses many long, complex sentences.

Ask the children to find examples of complex sentences and read them aloud. Make sure they follow the punctuation and maintain the sense, particularly when reading sentences with a number of clauses or more sophisticated punctuation, e.g. semi-colon; commas for parenthesis.

• How are some of the sentences constructed (e.g. using connectives) and what punctuation is used to separate the parts?

Use examples to look at how sentences can be reordered for effect, e.g. *'With no thought for the anger of Zeus ...'; 'When it lay lifeless on the ground ...'*

If we were retelling this part of the story for younger children, how might we change it? *Simplify the language; include less gory details.*

Challenge

Collect words and phrases from the text and make a glossary of formal and archaic language which could be used in their own writing later.

Turn back to **Respond and return** on page 12

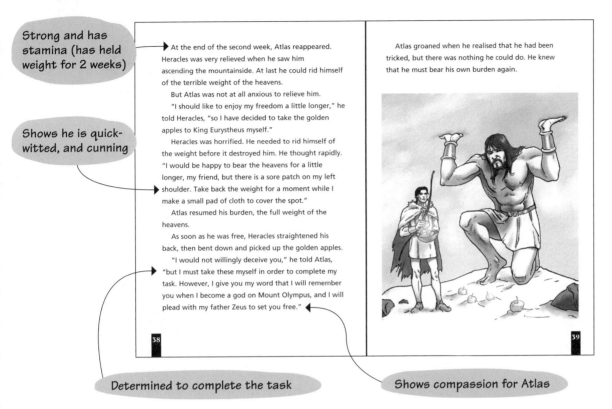

Strong and has stamina (has held weight for 2 weeks)

Shows he is quick-witted, and cunning

Determined to complete the task

Shows compassion for Atlas

Pages 38 and 39 AF 3

- What does this part of the story show about the character of Heracles? (See annotations.)

- How do we know that the events are told from Heracles' point of view? *The story follows him; shows his thoughts and feelings*

- Ask the children to look for evidence of what Heracles is thinking and feeling at different points in this scene, e.g. when Atlas first reappears *relieved*; when Atlas suggests taking the golden apples himself *horrified*; once he was free and Atlas is back bearing the burden *relieved, but guilty*

Ask the children to take on the role of Heracles and to speak aloud, using evidence in the text as the basis for their ideas.

Look for clues about how Atlas felt and what he might have been thinking and feeling at these same points.

- Which word suggests his feelings? *'Groaned'*

Ask the children to take on the role of Atlas and speak his thoughts and feelings aloud. Ask volunteers to retell the event from Atlas' point of view. Can they make the listeners feel really sorry for Atlas?

Challenge

Ask the children to write questions to ask either of the characters about this event, and then take turns to answer them in role.

◀ Turn back to **Respond and return** on page 13

Name: _____   **Date:** _____

Part 1

What qualities does Heracles show in this story? Tick the box and record your evidence.

	Not at all	A little	Yes	When?
Strong				
Clever				
Determined				
Kind/ compassionate				
Brave				
Honourable				
Proud				
Hasty/impulsive				
Selfish				

Part 2

Which three qualities listed above were most important for Heracles to succeed in his task? Why? Rank them in order and explain your choices.

Heracles the Hero: **The Golden Apples of the Hesperides** Skill: Analysing a character

Name: _____ **Date:** _____

Read page 13 again. Write about the meeting between Atlas and Heracles from Atlas' point of view. How might Atlas feel when he first sees Heracles? What might he do?

_____

_____

_____

_____

_____

_____

_____

_____

_____

_____

_____

_____

_____

_____

_____

_____

_____

_____

Genre: Greek legend
Suggested Renewed Framework
Unit: Traditional stories, fables, myths, legends
Author: Antonia Barber
Illustrator: Peter Doherty

Key Teaching Objectives

Session 1 / 2
Y5 Strand 7: 1 Use evidence from the text to explain ideas
Y5 Strand 8: 2 Compare usefulness of visualisation/ prediction/empathy in exploring texts

Session 3 / 4
Y5 Strand 7: 2 Infer writers' perspectives
Y5 Strand 7: 5 Explore how writer's produce dramatic effects
Y5 Strand 9: 4 Use direct/ reported speech, action and detail to vary pace/develop viewpoint

At a Glance

Session 1 / 2: Focus on Inference
Session 3 / 4: Focus on Language

This story tells of the twelfth and final task given to Heracles. The story offers opportunities for children to make inferences about the characters from their actions.

The story also contains vivid descriptions of the Underworld, land of the dead, and a strong build up to the final confrontation.

Independent Reading

Read and note the main events to compare them with predictions.

Session 1 / 2

Text introduction: prediction/activating prior knowledge
Pages 43 and 60

Recap the previous tasks Heracles has been given, and discuss why this final task is so important. Read the title and turn to page 60 to discover the final task. What do they think is the Underworld? Discuss their predictions about what complications/dangers there might be to overcome.

Teaching strategies
Pages 43–52

To establish that the children have understood the plot, ask them to contribute to a group retelling of the story so far.

AF 2

The following can be used to gather evidence for AF 2, where appropriate:
- What evidence can you find on pages 43 and 44 to show that Eurytheus is not a worthy king?
- What evidence do you have from the other stories to back up your opinion?
- What further evidence do you find of Heracles' bravery/ cleverness/kindness (or persistence) in this story?
- It says Heracles 'enthralled' the king and queen. What does this suggest about his character?

Going deeper: visualising AF 2

Ask the children to find and note words and phrases that help them to visualise the Underworld. As well as helping us visualise, what else do these details add to the story? *They build up the suspense; establish a threatening mood; add sense of fear*

Challenge: text-structure analysis

Ask the children to contribute to a problem and resolution chart to show the series of problems Heracles has on his journey through the Underworld and how they are overcome.

▶ Focus on: Inference • Pages 43 and 49

Respond and return: prediction
Page 53

Compare the actual events with the children's predictions. Discuss the challenge facing Heracles. Ask the children to predict how Heracles might persuade Cerberus to go with him using their knowledge of the story and Heracles' many skills and abilities. Will he succeed? How will Eurytheus react? How do you think the story will end?

Challenge: interpretive strategies

Write thought statements for King Hades deciding what to do about Heracles' request.

Follow-up

PCM 5 Part 1: children answer questions about the story
Challenge Part 1; Part 2: children make a storyboard

Text introduction: monitoring understanding
Page 53

Ask children to use their notes to recap Heracles' journey so far. Discuss how the story is gradually moving towards the big confrontation with Cerberus. Recap predictions from the previous session about how Heracles might succeed in his task.

Teaching strategies
Pages 54–59

To establish that the children have understood the plot, ask them to contribute to a group retelling of the story.

AF 6

The following can be used to gather evidence for AF 6, where appropriate:
- Which qualities does Heracles use to complete the final task? Why is this important?
- Does the writer want us to feel sorry for Eurystheus at the end? What makes you say that?
- 'The hero in a legend must be a character that the reader admires.' Did the writer achieve this?

Going deeper: text-structure analysis   AF 4
Identify the climax of the story where Heracles tackles the great hound Cerberus and talk about how the author 'lightens the mood' once he has been won over. Identify humorous details where Cerberus acts like a normal dog.

Challenge: discussion
Discuss whether it might be possible to make Cerberus a more sympathetic character, e.g. presenting things from his point of view.

 ## Focus on: Language • Pages 54–55   AF 5

Respond and return: interpretive strategies

Introduce the following discussion starters to reflect on the theme and characters of the story.
- Heracles is the greatest hero in any legend.
- Eurystheus deserved to be humiliated.
- Heracles has earned his place with the gods.
- We can all learn from the way Heracles achieved his goal.
Encourage the children to give reasons for their answers.

Challenge: activating prior knowledge
Compare Heracles with heroes in other legends and other types of story. How are they the same and different?

Follow-up

PCM 6 Part 1: write about the capture of Cerberus
Challenge Part 1; Part 2: write a brief description of Heracles' life so far

Synopsis

This story tells of Heracles' final task. Eurytheus gives Heracles the most terrible task he can think of: to bring back Cerberus, the huge three-headed dog that guards the gates to the land of the dead. The story shows how Heracles completes his final task through courage and guile.

Success Criteria

- I can look for evidence about characters and give my responses to them.
- I can empathise with characters to help me infer (work out) thoughts, feelings and motives.
- I can predict, visualise and imagine events as I read a story.
- I can say how writers create dramatic and humorous effects.
- I can describe events from another character's point of view, including details and actions.

Assessment Focus

AF 2*
AF 3
AF 4
AF 5
AF 6*

Further Writing

Make up a 13th labour for Heracles. Plan and write the story using a formal storytelling style.

Page 43 AF 3

Discuss the children's opinions of Eurystheus.
- What does this tell us about Eurystheus at this moment in the story?
- What are we told about the King? *He was jealous of Heracles; wants him to fail*
- What we can infer from what is said, e.g. signs that he is now desperate? (See annotations.)

Explain that you want the children to try to empathise with the character to explore fully his thoughts, feelings and motives at this point in the story.

Ask children to take on the role of Eurystheus and complete thought statements, e.g. *What I really hope …; The very worst thing would be …; I feel … because …; What if …; Perhaps I could …*

Encourage others to listen and say if they agree, referring to evidence in the text.

Concerned and compassionate

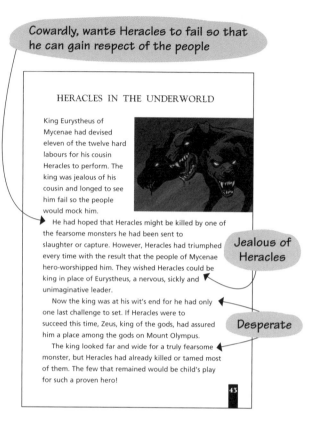

Cowardly, wants Heracles to fail so that he can gain respect of the people

HERACLES IN THE UNDERWORLD

King Eurystheus of Mycenae had devised eleven of the twelve hard labours for his cousin Heracles to perform. The king was jealous of his cousin and longed to see him fail so the people would mock him.

Jealous of Heracles

He had hoped that Heracles might be killed by one of the fearsome monsters he had been sent to slaughter or capture. However, Heracles had triumphed every time with the result that the people of Mycenae hero-worshipped him. They wished Heracles could be king in place of Eurystheus, a nervous, sickly and unimaginative leader.

Now the king was at his wit's end for he had only one last challenge to set. If Heracles were to succeed this time, Zeus, king of the gods, had assured him a place among the gods on Mount Olympus.

Desperate

The king looked far and wide for a truly fearsome monster, but Heracles had already killed or tamed most of them. The few that remained would be child's play for such a proven hero!

43

Page 49

Discuss the children's opinions of Heracles.
- What do his actions tell us about Heracles? (See annotations.)
- Do you think he was brave or foolish to release Theseus?

Explain that you want the children to try to empathise with Heracles to explore fully his thoughts, feelings and motives at this point in the story.
- What clues are there in the text about feelings? *Took pity on Theseus; slashed the ropes; quickly passed on*
- What are Heracles' inner thoughts at different points in the scene: when he sees Theseus; when he releases him; when he decides to move on?

Discuss the inner conflict at the line 'King Hades grows angry'. Role play one inner voice giving reasons why he should stay and help; another giving reasons why he should move on.

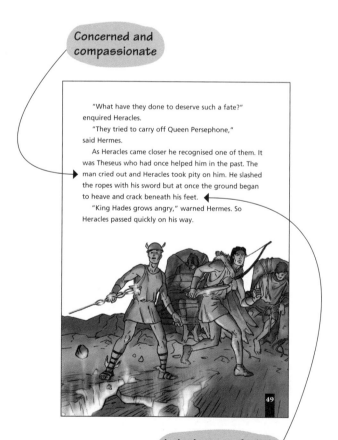

"What have they done to deserve such a fate?" enquired Heracles.

"They tried to carry off Queen Persephone," said Hermes.

As Heracles came closer he recognised one of them. It was Theseus who had once helped him in the past. The man cried out and Heracles took pity on him. He slashed the ropes with his sword but at once the ground began to heave and crack beneath his feet.

"King Hades grows angry," warned Hermes. So Heracles passed quickly on his way.

49

Is he brave or foolish to release Theseus?

Challenge

Ask children to create an inner monologue for Eurytheus or Heracles to fit into the relevant point in the story.

Turn back to **Respond and return** on page 18

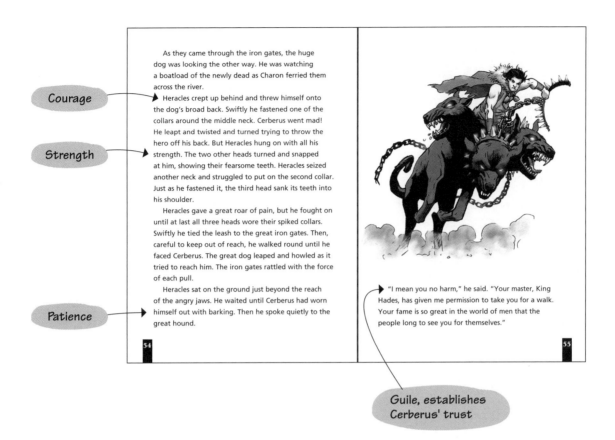

Courage →

As they came through the iron gates, the huge dog was looking the other way. He was watching a boatload of the newly dead as Charon ferried them across the river.

Heracles crept up behind and threw himself onto the dog's broad back. Swiftly he fastened one of the collars around the middle neck. Cerberus went mad! He leapt and twisted and turned trying to throw the hero off his back. But Heracles hung on with all his

Strength →

strength. The two other heads turned and snapped at him, showing their fearsome teeth. Heracles seized another neck and struggled to put on the second collar. Just as he fastened it, the third head sank its teeth into his shoulder.

Heracles gave a great roar of pain, but he fought on until at last all three heads wore their spiked collars. Swiftly he tied the leash to the great iron gates. Then, careful to keep out of reach, he walked round until he faced Cerberus. The great dog leaped and howled as it tried to reach him. The iron gates rattled with the force of each pull.

Patience →

Heracles sat on the ground just beyond the reach of the angry jaws. He waited until Cerberus had worn himself out with barking. Then he spoke quietly to the great hound.

54

"I mean you no harm," he said. "Your master, King Hades, has given me permission to take you for a walk. Your fame is so great in the world of men that the people long to see you for themselves."

55

Guile, establishes Cerberus' trust

Pages 54 and 55

Ask one of the children to read pages 54–55 aloud, using their voice appropriately while the others visualise the events.

Discuss how the author builds up to Heracles surprise 'assault' on Cerberus.

- How is the sense of sudden surprise created? *The dog looking the other way; choice of verbs and adverbs ('crept up', 'swiftly'); exclamation ('Cerberus went mad!')*
- Which words and phrases make Cerberus sound like a frightening beast that only Heracles could deal with? *'Broad back'; 'fearsome teeth'*

- How does the writer create a sense of a tremendous battle between them? *Describing the events in detail; use of action verbs, e.g. 'leapt', 'twisted', 'turned', 'struggled'*

Discuss how the atmosphere changes afterwards, e.g. Heracles sits and waits; speaks quietly and kindly.
- What skills is he using now?

Challenge

Ask the children to retell the event as if they are Heracles, including thoughts and feelings.

◄ Turn back to **Respond and return** on page 19

Part I

Answer the questions, referring to the text. Continue your answers overleaf if necessary.

1 What was Heracles' final task set by Eurystheus?

_____

2 Why did Eurystheus want Heracles to fail at his final task?

_____

3 'Only Hermes could pass freely between Olympus, Earth and the Underworld.' In your own words, write a brief synopsis of each of these places.

a) Olympus _____

_____

b) The Underworld _____

_____

4 'Their road took them to distant, rugged mountains.' Why does the author use the word 'rugged' in this sentence?

_____

5 How did Heracles feel when he saw Theseus on the Seats of Forgetfulness?

_____

_____

6 How do you think the story will continue?

_____

_____

Part 2

Make a storyboard to show how you think Heracles will get Cerberus to the living world.

© Pearson Education Ltd, 2010

Name: _____   **Date:** _____

Part 1

Imagine you are Heracles, and you are writing an account of how you captured Cerberus to send to King Hades. Remember to add details which show your character and feelings, as well as what you did.

_____

_____

_____

_____

_____

_____

_____

_____

_____

_____

_____

_____

_____

_____

_____

_____

_____

_____

_____

_____

_____

_____

_____

_____

Part 2

Write a brief description of Heracles' life so far. Include key events.

Levelling Guidance Sheets

The Levelling Guidance sheets have been developed to help you gather evidence on children's reading, and link this through to the Assessment Focuses (AFs). The Levelling Guidance sheets can be used periodically to assess children's progression in reading, helping you to identify gaps in their learning and inform planning and teaching. Each sheet offers example responses at two levels, appropriate to the text and year group.

Gathering reading assessment during guided reading

Choose the Levelling Guidance sheet for the chosen *Navigator* guided reading book, selecting the relevant story and session. Ensure this is at the appropriate level for the child or group of children you wish to assess, and conduct your guided reading session just as normal. When you come to the set of boxed questions in the teaching sessions these will be on the sheet. You can make notes on the responses the children give or circle the exemplified responses on the sheet. When the guided reading session has finished, you can review their responses, using the 'Grid Reference' to help link the child's response to the terminology on the Reading

Assessment Guidelines grid (see page 31). In this way, the Levelling Guidance sheets will help you to relate children's answers in guided reading to the National Curriculum Levels, as laid out in the Reading Assessment Guidelines. In doing this, over time, you can collect evidence for children's progress within the National Curriculum Levels across the AFs.

It may be that you wish to assess against an alternative Assessment Focus in a particular teaching session. Other assessment opportunities are identified in the teaching sessions by the AF symbol, and summarised on page 3. These, however, are not accompanied by Levelling Guidance sheets.

The sheets give examples of responses across the whole range of AFs. However, please note, the exemplified responses matched to levels of attainment are provided only as a guide. As always, professional judgement must be used when assessing children's learning progression, and a range of evidence should be gathered for each AF. It is important to have enough evidence against each AF, to help build up a picture of whether a child's reading skills are independent, consistent and embedded.

How Heracles Cleaned the Stables of King Augeus

Reading group names: _____ **Date:** _____

The following is based on the Reading Assessment Guidelines: Level 3 and 4.

Main Assessment Focus: AF 4 (Identify and comment on the structure and organisation of texts, including grammatical and presentational features at text level)

	Questions	Exemplified Responses	Reference	Notes
Pages 5–7	Why does the writer start with the introduction rather than going straight into the first story?	*To set the scene; to tell us who the characters are*	Level 3	
		Because it helps explain who the characters are; tells us about the twelve trials and why Heracles has to do them	Level 4/bullet 1	
Pages 9–14	Before describing the fifth task, the writer tells us about tasks 1 to 4. Why do you think this is?	*To introduce the new story; to fill in what has happened before*	Level 3	
		To show Heracles' strength; to build up to the new task	Level 4/bullet 1	
Pages 62–63	How does the layout make the pronunciation guide easy to use?	*It's in alphabetical order, columns*	Level 3	
		So you can quickly find the name; look across to see how to say it	Level 4/bullet 2	
Pages 60–61	What is the purpose of pages 60–61?	*It gives a list of all the trials Heracles had to do*	Level 3	
		It summarises all 12 tasks and shows where the stories fit in.	Level 4/bullet 1	

To achieve level 4, children should include more specific comments.

Reading group names: _____ **Date:** _____

The following is based on the Reading Assessment Guidelines: Level 3 and 4.

Main Assessment Focus: AF 5 (Explain and comment on writers' use of language, including grammatical and literary features at word and sentence level)				
	Questions	**Exemplified Responses**	**Reference**	**Notes**
Page 16	Which words and phrases suggest that you are reading a story set a long time ago?	_The kingdom of Elis; King Augeus_	Level 3	
		The innkeeper; his beasts	Level 4/bullet 1	
Pages 16–19	Read the dialogue between characters. Which parts suggest that this is not a modern story?	_'No man could clean it now'_	Level 3	
		People don't speak like that now; we wouldn't say that; it sounds really formal	Level 4/bullet 2	
Pages 16–20	How does the choice of words help to introduce the horror of the stables?	_'Foul stench'; 'stables (are) many feet deep in dung'_	Level 3	
		The writer contrasts the beautiful valley with the stench of the stables	Level 4/bullet 1	

To achieve level 4, children should be able to find a number of examples from the text.

Reading group names: _____ **Date:** _____

The following is based on the Reading Assessment Guidelines: Level 3 and 4.

	Questions	Exemplified Responses	**Reference**	**Notes**
Main Assessment Focus: AF 7 (Relate texts to their social, cultural and historical traditions)				
Pages 25–26	How could you tell this was a legend just from reading pages 25–26?	*Characters: the great hero and evil enemy; familiar opening where hero is set an 'impossible' task*	Level 3/bullet 2	
		Gods and goddesses; fantastical creatures; story will follow how he achieves the task	Level 4/bullet 1	
	How does the pattern of the story compare to the first story?	*Given a task; sets off on a journey*	Level 3/bullet 1	
		Longer, more complex; there are many problems to solve along the way; people have to help him	Level 4/bullet 1	
	How are the characters different in this story?	*In the first story the characters were all human; there are gods and goddesses in this story*	Level 3/bullet 2	
		Gods, goddesses; water nymphs play an important part in this story whereas in the first story the characters Heracles met were human	Level 4/bullet 1	

To achieve level 4, children should recognise a number of features from the text.

Reading group names: _____ **Date:** _____

The following is based on the Reading Assessment Guidelines: Level 3 and 4.

Main Assessment Focus: AF 4 (Identify and comment on the structure and organisation of texts, including grammatical and presentational features at text level)				
	Questions	**Exemplified Responses**	**Reference**	**Notes**
Pages 25–42	How is this story like a quest?	*There's a long journey and it tells you what happens along the way*	Level 3	
		The hero is searching for something; it involves a journey, and lots of trials along the way	Level 4/bullet 1	
Pages 25–42	Which words and phrases show how long the story takes?	*'A week passed'; 'At the end of the second week'*	Level 3	
		Time phrases identified from whole text	Level 4/bullet 2	
Pages 25–42	How is the structure of the story the same as the first story?	*The challenge is set up at the beginning; Heracles succeeds*	Level 3	
		Similar opening; sets an impossible task; problem solved through his efforts; it's longer, more complicated with more challenges	Level 4/bullet 2	
Page 34	Why is the meeting with Atlas important in the story?	*Only he could fetch the golden apples*	Level 3	
		So Heracles can complete his task	Level 4/bullet 1	

To achieve level 4, children should refer to examples from the whole text.

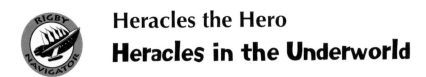
Reading group names: _____ **Date:** _____

The following is based on the Reading Assessment Guidelines: Level 3 and 4.

Main Assessment Focus: AF 2 (Understand, describe, select or retrieve information, events or ideas from texts and use quotation and reference to text)

	Questions	Exemplified Responses	Reference	Notes
Pages 43, 44	What evidence can you find on pages 43 and 44 to show that Eurytheus is not a worthy king?	*The people preferred Heracles*	Level 3/bullet 1	
		It says 'nervous, sickly and unimaginative leader' – these words all mean he was really weak	Level 4/bullet 2	
	What evidence do you have from the other stories to back up your opinion?	*He was scared by the wild boar*	Level 3/bullet 1	
		He jumped in the jar to escape the wild boar and everyone laughed; he was too terrified to take the apples and ran to his bedroom	Level 4/bullet 2	
Pages 46–51	What further evidence do you find of Heracles' bravery/ cleverness/kindness (or persistence) in this story?	*He sets Theseus free – that shows he's kind*	Level 3/bullet 2	
		Page 48 shows his cleverness; page 46 shows his bravery	Level 4/bullet 2	
Page 52	It says Heracles 'enthralled' the king and queen. What does this suggest about his character?	*He's charming as well*	Level 3/bullet 2	

To achieve level 4, children should refer to a number of points from the text.

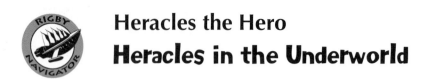

Reading group names: _____ **Date:** _____

The following is based on the Reading Assessment Guidelines: Level 3 and 4.

Main Assessment Focus: AF 6 (Identify and comment on writers' purposes and viewpoints and the overall effect on the reader)				
	Questions	**Exemplified Responses**	**Reference**	**Notes**
Pages 45–57	Which qualities does Heracles use to complete the final task? Why is this important?	_Courage, strength, patience; to show he is a good hero_	Level 3/bullet 1	
		He's a true hero, so needs other qualities as well as strength	Level 4/bullet 1	
Pages 58–59	Does the writer want us to feel sorry for Eurystheus at the end? What makes you say that?	_No, because he acts like a fool_	Level 3/bullet 2	
		The writer makes us laugh at him by showing him running to his bedroom	Level 4/bullet 3	
	'The hero in a legend must be a character that the reader admires.' Did the writer achieve this?	_Yes, he's brave to do all those tasks_	Level 3/bullet 1	
		Yes, because he showed he was clever as well as brave; the way he describes the challenges makes them seem impossible	Level 4/bullet 3	

To achieve level 4, children should show awareness of the writer's viewpoint.

Reading Assessment Guidelines: levels 3 and 4

Pupil name .... Class/Group .... Date ....

	AF1 – use a range of strategies, including accurate decoding of text, to read for meaning	AF2 – understand, describe, select or retrieve information, events or ideas from texts and use quotation and reference to text	AF3 – deduce, infer or interpret information, events or ideas from texts	AF4 – identify and comment on the structure and organisation of texts, including grammatical and presentational features at text level	AF5 – explain and comment on writers' use of language, including grammatical and literary features at word and sentence level	AF6 – identify and comment on writers' purposes and viewpoints, and the overall effect of the text on the reader	AF7 – relate texts to their social, cultural and historical traditions
Level 4		**Across a range of reading** • some relevant points identified • comments supported by some generally relevant textual reference or quotation, e.g. reference or motive from their actions at different points • inferences often correct, but comments are not always rooted securely in the text or repeat narrative or content	**Across a range of reading** • comments make inferences based on evidence from different points in the text, e.g. interpreting a character's first and then goes back to tell you why the child was in the road' • some basic features of writer's use of language identified, e.g. 'the writer uses bullet points for the main reasons'	**Across a range of reading** • some structural choices identified with simple comment, e.g. 'he describes the accident first and then goes back to tell you why the child was in the road' • simple comments on some basic features of writer's use of language, e.g. "disgraceful" is a good word	**Across a range of reading** • some basic features of writer's use of language identified, e.g. 'all the questions make you want to find out what happens next' • simple comments on writer's choices, e.g. "disgraceful" is a good word	**Across a range of reading** • main purpose identified, e.g. 'it's all about why going to the dentist is important and how you should look after your teeth' • simple comments show some awareness of writer's viewpoint, e.g. 'he only tells you good things about the farm and makes the shop sound boring' • simple comment on overall effect on reader, e.g. 'the way she describes him as "ratlike" and "shitty" makes you think he's disgusting'	**Across a range of reading** • features common to different texts or versions of the same text identified, with simple comment, e.g. characters, settings, presentational features • simple comment on writer's context has on the meaning of texts, e.g. historical context, place, social relationships
Level 3	**In most reading** • range of strategies used mostly effectively to read with fluency, understanding and expression	**In most reading** • simple, most obvious points identified though there may also be some misunderstanding, e.g. about information from different places in the text • some comments include quotations from or references to text, but not always relevant, e.g. often retelling or paraphrasing sections of the text rather than using it to support comment	**In most reading** • straightforward inference based on a single point of reference in the text, e.g. 'he was upset because it says "he was crying"' • responses to text show meaning established at a literal level e.g. '"walking good" means "walking carefully"' or based on personal speculation e.g. a response based on what they personally would be feeling rather than feelings of character in the text	**In most reading** • a few basic features of organisation at text level identified, with little or no linked comment, e.g. 'it tells about all the different things you can do at the zoo'	**In most reading** • a few basic features of writer's use of language identified, but with little or no comment, e.g. 'there are lots of adjectives' or 'he uses speech marks to show there are lots of people there'	**In most reading** • comments identify main purpose, e.g. 'the writer doesn't like violence' • express personal response but with little awareness of writer's viewpoint or effect on reader, e.g. 'she was just horrible like my nan is sometimes'	**In most reading** • some simple connections between texts identified, e.g. similarities in plot, topic, or books by same author, about same characters • recognition of some features of the context of texts, e.g. historical setting, social or cultural background

Key: BL – Below level   IE – Insufficient evidence

		Low 3	Secure 3	High 3	Low 4	Secure 4	High 4
IE							
BL							

Overall assessment (tick one box only)

© Crown Copyright 2010. Reproduced under the terms of the Click-Use Licence.

Rigby
Halley Court, Jordan Hill, Oxford, OX2 8EJ

Rigby is an imprint of Pearson Education Limited, a company incorporated in England
and Wales, having its registered office at Edinburgh Gate, Harlow, Essex, CM20 2JE.
Registered company number: 872828

www.rigbyed.co.uk

Rigby is a registered trademark of Reed Elsevier, Inc, licensed to Pearson Education
Limited

Text © Pearson Education Limited 2010
Cover © Pearson Education Limited 2010
Reading Assessment guidelines © Crown copyright 2010. Reproduced under the terms
of the Click-Use Licence.

First published 2010

14 13 12 11 10
10 9 8 7 6 5 4 3 2 1

British Library Cataloguing in Publication Data is available from the British Library on
request.

ISBN 978 0 433 002 39 0

Written by Carol Matchett
Typeset by Andrew Magee Design
Cover design by Ian Lansley at Dickidot
Printed in the UK by Henry Ling

Every effort has been made to contact copyright holders of material reproduced in
this book. Any omissions will be rectified in subsequent printings if notice is given
to the publishers.